Stamping
IN A WEEKEND

Stamping

IN A WEEKEND

Beautiful ways to decorate paper, fabric, wood and ceramics

JULIET BAWDEN

NH
NEW
HOLLAND

Happy 40th Birthday Carol

First published in the UK in 1996 by
New Holland (Publishers) Ltd
London • Cape Town • Sydney • Singapore

24 Nutford Place, London W1H 6DQ UK
P.O. Box 144, Cape Town 8000, South Africa
3/2 Aquatic Drive, Frenchs Forest, NSW 2086, Australia

ISBN 1 85368 722 7 (hbk)
ISBN 1 85368 723 5 (pbk)

Editor: Emma Callery
Designer: Peter Crump
Photographer: Shona Wood

Editorial Direction: Yvonne McFarlane

Reproduction by Hirt and Carter (Pty) Ltd
Printed and bound by Times Offset (M) Sdn. Bhd.

Acknowledgment
The author and the publishers would like to thank the following
people for their help in making this book: My assistant Labeena
Ishaque for all her hard work and the cover illustration, Shona
Wood for her wonderful photography, Jo Ryde for her hand
modelling, Emma Callery for being so cheerful and Yvonne
McFarlane for her giggles.

Important:
Every effort has been made to present clear and accurate
instructions. Therefore, the author and publishers can accept
no liability for any injury, illness or damage which may inadver-
tently be caused to the user whilst following these instructions.

CONTENTS

INTRODUCTION

6

INTRODUCTION

Stamping is an ideal weekend craft. You need very little in the way of equipment and it takes up little or no room. In fact, everything you need can be kept in a shoe box. It has become very popular in recent years and the paints, pens, pigments, embossing powders and stamps available are continually increasing. Because the hobby has become so popular, it means that stamps are readily available everywhere, ranging from tourist shops to toy emporiums and craft stores. However, making your own stamps has the advantages of being cheaper and unique. Among other things, they can be made from sponge, foam rubber, cork, vegetables, wood and linoleum, and at the beginning of this book I will show you how to use each of these materials (see pages 8-13).

The variety of artefacts to stamp upon is enormous and ranges from interiors including walls, floors and furniture to smaller-scale items such as boxes and other containers. In addition, you can stamp on clothing and accessories.

The art of stamping is taking a block with a pattern cut into or onto it, coating it with paint and then transferring the colour and pattern onto a background. It takes a bit of practice to get the knack of how much colour to apply and how hard to press the stamp. For example, you need to apply different amounts of pressure on, say, cloth as opposed to paper. Curved surfaces are more difficult, but not impossible to stamp, and stamps will slide on a shiny glazed surface. However, a brief bit of practice on these surfaces will soon mean that you are stamping with the best of them.

The beauty of this form of decorative paint technique is that the surfaces on which you can stamp need very little or no preparation whatsoever. The only surface that may need treating is bare wood which should be cleaned and sanded before stamping on it, as with any other type of painting. The other thing to check on is that you have the right type of paint for the surface on which you are stamping — so, use fabric paints, say, on items of clothing, and emulsion paint on wooden furniture or other wooden items (see also page 13). Apart from these small points, there really is nothing to stop you from starting stamping today.

From the moment that I started writing this book, any time anyone came into the work room they had to join in. Stamping is a completely compulsive activity, and great fun, too.

Happy stamping!

Juliet Bawden

GETTING STARTED

Simply designed stamps can be made with everyday objects so should you want to have a go today, find a potato, a knife and some felt-tipped pens and make a start. However, many stamps with more elaborate or detailed designs are also manufactured, giving you a wide range of styles from which to choose.

THE HISTORY OF STAMPING

Stamps and seals have been used for thousands of years and there still exist examples which can be cited such as a Babylonian seal from 4000BC, and from 3000BC a seal from Syria (or Ebla as it was then known). Before the twentieth century, the majority of people were unable to read or write and so seals were a convenient way to authenticate documents or letters. When one person wished to communicate with another, and could not write, a scribe would be employed to write the document and the author would then present their seal which would be stamped onto the material on which the missive was written. Every person would have a personal seal which was difficult to copy. Merchants would have a picture of their trade, while others had something representative of their occupation, and naturally there are examples of stamps using script in a decorative way.

The Chinese and Japanese still use seals more frequently than most other races, as they have done for thousands of years. This may be because the script used by these nationalities lends itself naturally to seal designs. There are examples that can be seen today from Ancient Egypt and from Roman times in the British Museum. The Papal Bull is, in fact, a lead seal.

Seals and stamps were made from a variety of materials such as stone, wood, ivory and metals, even gold or silver, and many of the original, oldest examples were made from clay or bone. Seals were also formed in a variety of shapes ranging from rectangular and square to oval and circular. The round shape still remains the most popular today. Many seals were cylindrical when all script was cuniform, as in the ancient languages of Mesopotamia and Persia. The seal was used by rolling it onto the surface of clay, which was then allowed to dry in the sun. Sometimes these slabs of clay would then be enclosed, like the letter of today, into an envelope — but at that time, the envelope would be made from clay as well.

Stamps used to be placed directly onto the surface of the document but gradually it evolved and seals were placed onto softened wax. Nowadays, wax seals are used on documents to give them a mark of officialdom but many ancient papers still survive where this method was used by people who often could not write despite eminent positions of authority. In fact, seals were sometimes preferred to inked signatures because of this official appearance. Most wealthy people would have their own signet rings which would be placed into the sealing wax and this was a common way of sealing envelopes and scrolls during the eighteenth and nineteenth centuries.

Today, stamps are often made from rubber. Placed straight onto paper, they are used for many different purposes — in offices, libraries, and for many official tasks. In the last decade there has been an upsurge in the variety of rubber stamps available for decorative purposes and for use by children at home. This book illustrates how to make stamps from rubber as well as from a variety of other materials such as polystyrene, linoleum, synthetic foam, fruit, torn newspaper, and sponges, as well as using more traditional wood and metal blocks.

SELECTING A MANUFACTURED STAMP

A traditional rubber stamp is made in three parts. The design (die) is cut from rubber, and this is laid onto a wooden handle (block) with a layer of foam (cushion) sandwiched between. When buying a rubber stamp it is worth checking certain features to make sure the stamp is easy to use and, most importantly, that the image will be clear once printed.

THE DIE
* Ensure that the design has been cut evenly and deeply. Those that are quite shallow will not produce a clear image, and those that are uneven will result in parts of the image not appearing. Whatever the material used for the design, it should be trimmed as closely to the edge of the design as possible.
* Some manufacturers produce polymer stamps which enable far more intricate designs to be realised. The advantage of this type of stamp is that fabric and acrylic paints are easily washed off with water, but the slight drawback is that

marker pens are not always successful.
* One other material used to make stamps is hardened plastic which can be quickly and efficiently inked. But they do not allow for any highly detailed design to be inscribed.

THE BLOCK

* It is very difficult to produce a clear print just by holding onto the design, so the handle is very important. It should not be overly large as there will then be a temptation to rock the stamp while printing resulting in an uneven or smeared image.
* Blocks can be made from a variety of materials but be wary of those made with soft materials such as foam or sponge. There might be a tendency to push down too much which will squash both the block and the design, again causing fuzziness.

THE CUSHION

* The cushions can either be trimmed to the shape of the outline of the design or they must be the same shape as the handle. When pressure is applied, check that it is only the design that touches the surface and not the lower edge of the handle. The depth of the cushion should therefore be checked before buying a stamp.

MOUNTING ADHESIVE

* The three parts of the stamp are held together with adhesive which is usually a rubber cement or a mounting film. Because inks are solvent-based and so will destroy the adhesive, eventually resulting in the stamp falling apart, cleaning stamps is important. Water-based products, such as some marker pens, cannot do any damage.

CARE OF STAMPS

1 To ensure that the die stays in good condition, always store all stamps with their rubber side down.
2 Some inks will stain the stamp even after cleaning, especially if using darker colours. However, as long as the stamp has been cleaned properly, this will not affect the quality of the print when the stamp is used again.

3 Stamps must be cleaned after use and when changing the colour.
4 After using water-based products, stamp the pad onto a piece of scrap paper or kitchen towel until only a vague impression is being made and then rinse under running water.
5 After using solvent-based inks, keep stamping until as little ink as possible is left — as for water-based products — and then dry them thoroughly. This should be sufficient but, if not, use a mix of water and washing-up liquid or other detergent and gently clean. It might be useful to have an old nail brush or toothbrush which can be used if there is a really stubborn stain.
6 Always clean stamps immediately. When this is impossible, stamp on to a scrap piece of paper to remove as much ink as you can and then place the stamp on a damp sponge or towel. The ink that is left will not dry as long as it is kept wet.
7 When ink has dried onto the stamp, dab solvent-based cleaner onto the die and gently scrub with a toothbrush.
8 Never immerse the whole stamp in water as this is quite unnecessary and can actually affect the adhesive used to make the stamp.

TOOLS AND EQUIPMENT

You will find that you already have much of the equipment needed for making stamps and for practising the art of stamping in your home. Many stamps, paints, inks, and materials on which to print can obviously be bought, but at first, it is advisable to experiment with what is already available as this will save a lot of time and expense.

MAKING A RUBBER STAMP

For the rubber you will need:
Rubber erasers
Tracing paper
Soft pencil
Fountain pen
Needle
Craft knife
Sandpaper
Scrap paper

1 Choose a rubber of a suitable size and work out a design. White rubber is preferable, and the less springy the better. For the design, either copy one of the templates from pages 76-8, or create your own pattern or picture.
2 Trace the image to be copied, or draw the design, heavily onto the tracing paper using the soft pencil. Then shade on top of all the heavier drawn lines until they are covered.
3 Turn the tracing paper over and hold it firmly in place on top of the rubber. Draw heavily on top of the lines of the design and this will then be transferred to the top of the rubber.
4 Use the fountain pen to go over the image, correcting any missed parts. The reversed image can now be seen more clearly, so making it easier to see while cutting out.
5 Slowly stroke the needle over the outline several times, allowing the surface of the rubber to be cut just a miniscule amount. Don't score a line immediately — just stroke gently. The angle of this initial scoring should be away from the image with no undercutting.
6 Now use the tip of a very sharp craft knife and cut the lines of the image a little deeper taking care to keep the angle of the cut sloping. The cut-away section should narrow towards the top like a sand dune.
7 Clean any excess ink from the rubber with a moistened tissue or baby wipe. Then place the stamp onto an ink pad and take a first print onto a smooth piece of paper. You will then be able to see where rough edges need to be trimmed and to generally check that the image is correct.
8 Trim excess rubber and any rough areas with the knife and then take another print to check. Repeat this process until a clear, satisfactory image is achieved. If there are any large areas in the design it may help to keep these clear by making deeper cuts in the rubber with the knife.
9 If small mistakes are not too deep, they can be corrected by using sandpaper to rub down the surface. If it is not possible to rectify an image, use the other side of the rubber and start again. Alternatively, if a rubber is large

enough, cut it into smaller sections or remove one part of a design if a mistake has been made.

For the block you will need:
Wood or dowelling to suit the stamp
Small saw
5 mm (¼ in)-thick cellulose sponge
Adhesive

1 Cut a suitable length of wood or dowelling to fit the back of the stamp. This should not overlap the stamp but it can be the same size or slightly smaller. It would be impossible to place the stamp accurately if the block is larger than the stamp, as the stamp cannot be seen if this happens.
2 Cut the cellulose sponge to the same shape as the stamp and then glue this to the back of the rubber stamp.
3 Next, glue the wooden handle to the back of the sponge.
4 Make a mark on the stamp or the handle to indicate which is the top of the image.

The stamp does not necessarily need a handle, but it is much easier to use and less messy if there is something to hold other than the stamp. Many offices have stamps which are no longer used, so if you can obtain some of these the

rubber can be stripped from the handle and the handle reused. Hoarded or waste objects such as cotton reels, small jars with lids, and plastic boxes, can also be used as handles.

For a more professional finish, either stamp the image onto the back of the handle or onto a piece of paper which is then glued onto the handle. Give it three coats of varnish and, when dry, glue the handle onto the rubber stamp.

STAMPS MADE USING OTHER MATERIALS

As long as the stamping medium will adhere to it, you can use any object as a stamp, whatever the shape or size, plain or patterned. Indian shops are a source of old fabric stamps; metal and wooden stamps can be sought from printers; biscuit cutters are a useful pre-cut tool, and patterned rubber rollers from decorators' outlets can be used, especially if a larger area needs to be covered. Inca-wheels (roller stamps that produce a continuous pattern) can be found in many shops nowadays, and make good presents for children as they are easy to use. They often have inter-changeable wheels so you can quickly vary the designs.

CORK

Cork can be bought in sheets of varying thicknesses or you can simply use cork matting. Transfer a design onto the cork surface in the same way as above, and then using a sharp craft knife, gradually cut out the image. Corks from bottles can also be used as stamping tools, either as circular stamps which will leave a patterned impression from the corks or a design can be cut from the side or top and the corks used in this way. Draw a design on the cork in pen or pencil ① and then carefully cut it out with a craft knife ②. The design should be fairly simple as the cork can be fiddly to cut away. You can also buy more detailed cork stamps ③.

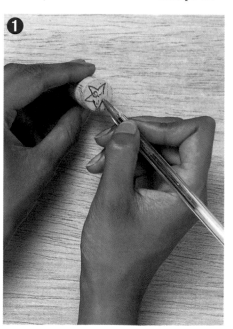

LINOLEUM

Linoleum is readily available from craft shops in standard sizes and it can be cut into different shapes with strong scissors. Draw your design directly onto the surface with a pencil which can be easily erased with a rubber. Specialist cutting tools can be bought from craft suppliers and there are numerous different shaped blades available. These are interchangeable so you need only purchase one handle. For information on making a lino cut, see the lino-cut bird on pages 18-19.

Once you are happy with your design, cut around it with the cutting tool ④. Then neaten the linoleum by trimmimg around the stamp with a sharp pair of scissors ⑤. Cover the image with an even coat of paint ⑥, and finally stamp ⑦.

FRUIT AND VEGETABLES

Fresh produce can be used for printing with the most wonderful results. There are innumerable fruits and vegetables that can be used, such as apples, lemons, hard plums, potatoes, turnips and carrots. When using the fruit or vegetable for its own imprint, citrus fruits and apples produce particularly interesting prints.

When cutting into the surface to create a pattern it is better to use a potato or other vegetable with a hard inner surface. Lino cutting tools can be used for gouging out the image required and, as stated above, there are many different blades available. Dried fruit

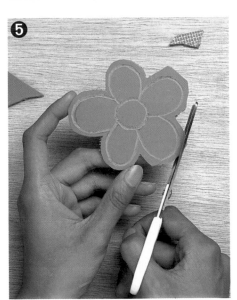

can also be used such as apple rings and pears ⑧. An interesting shape is particularly good for repeat patterns. To make a potato print, first clean the potato thoroughly and then cut it in half ⑨. Draw the shape onto the cut side of the potato using a felt-tipped pen ⑩. Then, using a craft knife, cut away the part of the design you do not want printed, so that the part you do want stands proud of the surface ⑪. Finally, paint colour onto the part standing proud and then print onto your surface ⑫.

POLYSTYRENE

Polystyrene trays that fresh meat and fish are placed in at supermarkets make excellent surfaces from which to print. A pencil, twig or any blunt tool can be used to make a picture or pattern on the polystyrene surface from which a print can then be taken. This is particularly successful with children who can create quite complicated patterns easily on this surface.

You can buy polystyrene ceiling or wall tiles that are often already patterned. The pattern can be used exactly as it is, or it can be cut into to make an image incorporating the pattern already in place ⑬.

SPONGE

Sponges come in pre-cut shapes or you can cut out the shape required from a sheet of sponge. It is easier to use thin sponge as thicker ones tend to be rather messy. To get a good print from sponge it is best to apply only a thin layer of ink and not to press too hard.
It is also possible to use compressed sponge, but be careful about allowing this to become wet as it will expand. It is best to mount compressed sponge on a handle.

To cut a stamp from a piece of sponge first draw the design onto a piece of sponge using a felt tipped pen ⑭. Then carefully cut it out using scissors ⑮.

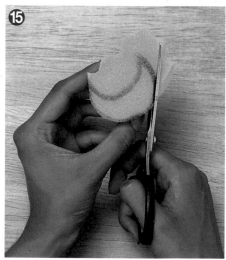

SCRUNCHED PAPER

Scrunched and torn paper make interesting impressions when used as stamps. Whole walls in rooms have been printed in this way, yet at the other end of the scale, wonderful cards and wrapping papers can also be created using this method of stamping.

WOOD

Wood can be carved to make a die though it should be noted that wooden stamps are more successful if the image stands out from the block as opposed to being indented. It is difficult to produce a clear image if it is indented because of the nature of the material.

You can buy a variety of wooden stamps from many outlets — and wooden stamps that newspaper and magazine printers used are often to be found in antique and junk shops.

STAMPING MEDIUM

The surface on which you are going to stamp determines the kind of ink that will be used. Most fluids can be used as inks as long as they can be applied to the die and will adhere to the material on which the stamp is to be placed. Traditionally, you would buy an ink pad inked with a pre-selected colour and once the pad is dry it can be re-inked. However, a whole variety of media can now be used and is readily available so consult the lables on all containers to see what is the most appropriate product for your project.

INK

Inks can be permanent on non-permanent and this should be noted when purchasing the product. It is always easier to use a stamp pad for these inks ① and it is possible to make one using layers of felt covered with muslin. This should be placed in a container with a lid which will keep the pad damp, preventing the ink from drying up. Bottles of ink are available from stationers and art suppliers in a multitude of colours. The pads are best stored upside down to keep the ink at the surface.

FELT-TIPPED PENS

Felt-tipped pens are produced with permanent and non-permanent inks, water-based and solvent-based. Experiment to find out which adheres best to which materials. The advantage of using felt-tipped pens is that different areas of the design can be coloured with a variety of colours, so once stamped, a multi-coloured image will appear on the surface of the material.

PAINTS

Most paints can be used for printing, whether they are powder, ink or poster paints ②. Usually the thicker the paint, the better the result as the colour will be more vibrant.

A wide range of emulsion paint is now available in small quantities and you can also have colours made up. This type of paint produces some wonderful effects and, again, sections of a stamp can be painted in different colours before stamping.

GENERAL TIPS BEFORE STAMPING

1 Ensure that the work surface on which you are stamping is flat and hard.

2 Make sure that all materials on which you are printing are flat, removing creases if working with fabric and use masking tape to keep other products in place. This will help you to concentrate on the stamping rather than attempting to keep the paper or fabric still as well! When stamping onto a box, lampshade, or similar, secure the object as well as you can before starting to stamp.

3 Always test the stamp on a scrap of paper or material first as this is the only chance you will have to rectify any problems that might occur with either the die or the medium being used.

4 Do not over-ink the stamp as the result will be a smudged image. When using an ink pad, lightly tap the stamp on the surface, do not press down hard. If using a brush to apply paint, make sure it has been gently stroked along the edge of the pot before brushing onto the image and ensure that the paint is applied evenly. It is worth noting that less ink is needed when the image is finely detailed.

5 Do not rock the stamp once on the surface as the image will blur. Larger stamps need firm pressure at the centre and while held in place, lighter pressure should be applied around the edges.

6 If you are using a second colour over the first stamp, always allow plenty of time for the first set of stamps to dry.

GIFTS FOR THE HOME

Gifts for the home includes both utilitarian and decorative objects. This is the ideal place to look for ideas for house warming presents, or just a gift to say thank you when you have been a weekend guest. Even something as simple as a bar of soap can be made into a special gift by wrapping it in plain brown paper and stamping a design on the paper. Flowerpots are inexpensive and can be easily stamped with a decoration. Choose a colour that fits in with the decor and buy or make a design that you know the person you are giving it to will like.

CERAMIC DAISY-STAMPED VASE

A simple dark blue ceramic vase looks as if it may be the easiest thing one could possibly stamp. However, with a curved and shiny surface, it can be difficult to stamp your image without it slipping about. The only advice for achieving the perfect stamp, is to practise before you try stamping your chosen piece. Or incorporate the sliding of the stamp and the imperfections into a pattern, layering the stamps one over another, as has been done here.

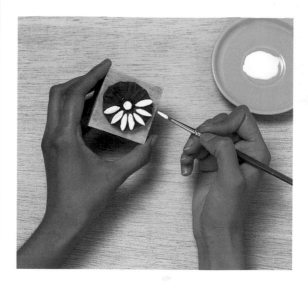

1 Making sure that the stamp is clean and dry, use the paintbrush to smoothly paint the entire stamp white. It is best to start at the centre of the stamp and work out to the edges.

YOU WILL NEED

Daisy stamp

Emulsion paints (white, yellow, red)

Paintbrush (fine)

Ceramic vase (blue)

Nail brush

VARIATIONS

Try alternating the colours of the flowers so that some of them are printed white on yellow; or how about just stamping the flowers around the rim of the pot?

2 Place the stamp onto the vase, press down firmly and roll across its surface so that the whole image is transferred onto the vase. Paint the stamp white again and repeat to cover the vase randomly in white daisies. Leave to dry.

3 Wash off the paint in warm water, using a nail brush to ensure all the crevices are clean; pat dry with a clean cloth and then paint only the petals of the daisy stamp with the yellow emulsion.

4 Stamp over the white daisies that are already there, so that the white shows through and the petals are yellow and white. Repeat to cover all the white flowers on the vase.

5 Clean off the stamp again, paint only the centre of the flower with the red emulsion and then stamp it into the centre of each daisy. Remember that it doesn't matter if the stamp slips slightly, as these imperfections can be incorporated into the pattern.

WOODEN CHAIR WITH BIRD LINO PRINTS

Lino cuts make unique stamps, and the design can be your own or copied from something that you like. The cutting made for this chair is of a little bird, which was cut to fit onto the width of the wooden slats. The effect from lino stamps is quite rough and earthy as the image is transferred in an uneven manner. But it can be touched up if you prefer a smooth finish.

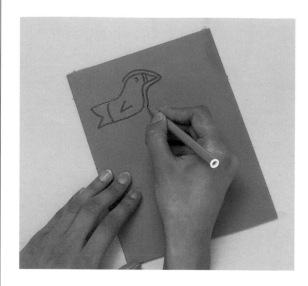

1 Remembering that the lines you draw will be in relief once they are stamped, draw a design onto the lino with your marker pen or pencil. The simpler your design, the stronger the stamped image will be. If you want to use the same bird design, transfer the template on page 77 onto the lino.

YOU WILL NEED

Small piece of lino

Fine marker pen (black) or a soft pencil

Bird template (page 77)

Lino cutter

Scissors or craft knife

Wooden chair

Paintbrush (fine)

Stamping paint (stone)

— VARIATIONS —

You will see from the photograph to the left, that birds have also been stamped on the seat of this slatted chair. Instead of repeating this triangular pattern, perhaps you could randomly scatter the birds across the seat, or make an arrow-head shape, as if for a flock of birds in flight.

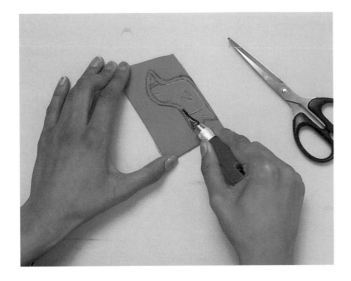

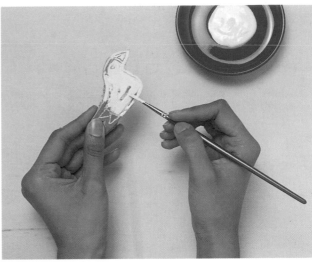

2 Carefully cut along the lines with the lino cutter. Hold the cutter firmly, with your thumb placed on the top of the handle, and push the cutter blade into the lino and push away from yourself. The lino will peel away as you do this. Then cut around the edge with the scissors or craft knife.

3 Using the paintbrush, paint the lino cutting with the stone coloured stamping paint. Make sure you don't overload the paintbrush with paint as it will make this process a little messy.

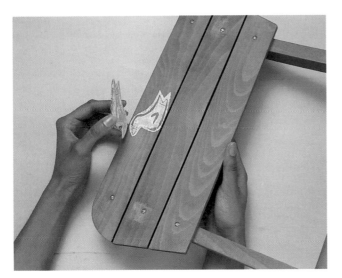

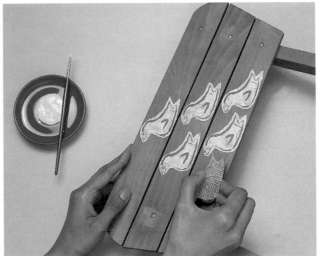

4 Place the lino cutting face down onto the chair where you wish to stamp it. Press it down firmly, especially around the edges pushing the cutting down here as they tend to rise outwards once they are damp. Lift off in one swift movement.

5 Repeat stamping to create a pattern of your choice, adding a fresh coat of paint each time. A triangular pattern like the one here is very simple and easy to do.

SHELL AND WAVE FRIEZE

Ideal for a bathroom, this frieze is made using two stamps in different shades of blue. Both the rhythm of the waves, and the way in which the shell neatly fits into the curls makes a very good composition. It is difficult to get an even colour when you first start stamping, so practise on a spare piece of paper until you feel you have achieved the density of paint you desire. If you do make mistakes you can always fill in gaps carefully using a paintbrush.

1 To mark out the area you will be working on the frieze, measure 3 cm (1½ in) in from the top and bottom edges of the border and rule off both sides with a pencil.

YOU WILL NEED

Border frieze
Ruler
Pencil
Stamping or acrylic paints (dark blue, light blue)
Paintbrush
Wave stamp
Shell stamp
Soft eraser

VARIATIONS

Modify this design to achieve very different effects by using different colourways. For example, sea green waves and golden shells look quite stunning, or substitute silver stars for the shells.

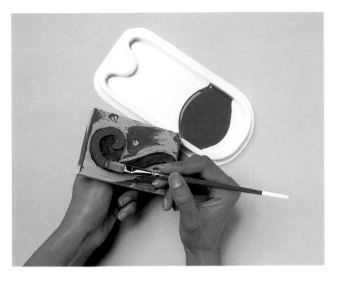

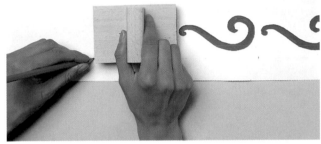

2 Pour the dark blue paint into a saucer or a tray and load the paintbrush with paint, but not overly so. Cover all of the wave stamp evenly with the paint from the paintbrush.

3 Working from right to left (or vice versa if you are left-handed), place the bottom edge of the stamp on the 3 cm (1½ in) line and press down firmly, rocking slightly from side to side, to impress the colour. While it is still on the paper, mark off the bottom left-hand corner (or right-hand corner) of the stamp block with a pencil to act as a positional guide.

4 Using the pencil mark, repeat step 3 stamping along to the end of the border. Leave to dry and then repeat on the top edge. If necessary, neaten the stamp prints with the paintbrush.

5 Take the shell stamp and cover it evenly with the light blue paint. Working in the same direction, place the bottom edge of the stamp block on the bottom edge of the border, and with the left side against the marks made in step 3. Press down firmly as before. Repeat along the top and bottom edges and then, if necessary, neaten the stamp prints with the paintbrush. When the paint is dry, rub out the pencil marks with the soft eraser.

SPONGE-STRIPED CUSHION

This wonderfully textured monochrome cushion is an unusual example of stamping, but it it so easy to do and very effective. Using an everyday bath sponge and brown wrapping paper the basic ingredients are swiftly to hand, making this an ideal stamping project for the first timer.

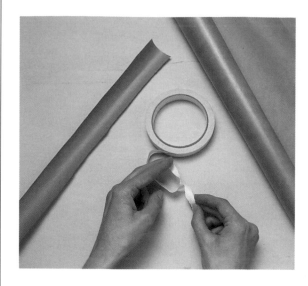

1 Cut the brown paper into strips that are about 7.5 cm (3 in) wide. Then take a length of masking tape and tear it down the middle to form two strips, both with one straight edge and one rough edge.

YOU WILL NEED

Brown paper
Scissors
Masking tape
White cotton fabric
Fabric paints (black, white)
Plastic container
Household sponge
Scrap paper

VARIATIONS

You can, of course, make the stripes any colour you like. A striking bright red or blue would look just as good. For more interesting colour mixes, try using a contrast colour other than white - all sorts of subtle shades will then be created as you work.

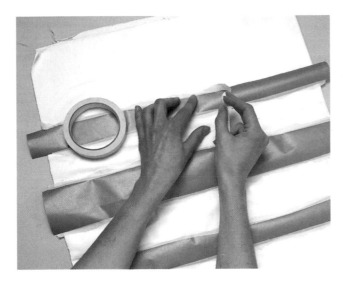

2 Cut two equal sized pieces from the cotton fabric. Next, place the paper onto one of the pieces (the cushion front) at equal distances apart and tape down the paper with the torn masking tape. Make sure that the torn edges face outwards onto the fabric. Don't feel that the lines have to be accurately straight; some variation in the lines adds to the textural interest of this cushion.

3 Pour small quantities of the black and white fabric paints into the plastic container, allowing them to mix slightly where the paints meet. Then take the household sponge and cover the surface evenly with the two paints, stamping off any excess onto scrap paper.

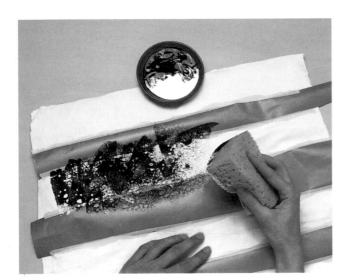

4 Stamp along the spaces on the cushion cover, created by the paper and tape. As you apply more paint to the sponge, you will find that the black will slowly change to charcoal and then to grey as the black and the white mix together. Make the most of this by going over some of the darker areas when the paint has become lighter, or use the part of the sponge that has more white on it. Repeat stamping until all the exposed fabric has been covered.

5 Leave the paint to dry and then slowly remove the tape and the newspaper to reveal the pattern beneath. If you want the back of your cushion to look the same as the front, repeat these steps on the second piece of fabric. To fix the paint, iron the fabric on the reverse side with a medium-hot iron. Then make up the cover. With right sides facing, stitch around three edges with a 12mm (½in) seam allowance. Insert a cushion pad and then neatly oversew the last seam to close the gap.

GIFTS FOR THE HOME GALLERY

Flowerpot
Ceramic is a difficult surface on which to stamp. It is easier to stamp onto earthenware as the stamp will not slide. On curved surfaces such as these, start with one side of the stamp and roll it over the surface and lift in one deft movement.

Soaps
Soap can be turned into a special gift by wrapping in plain brown, green and blue paper and stamping with a shell design.

Tiles
Bathroom tiles can either be stamped using gloss paint or with emulsion which is then given a protective coat of varnish.

Gift box
A small plywood box has the centre of a tile stamped onto its lid and a tiny pattern stamped round its sides.

Table mats

Easy to make table mats made from fringed hessian stamped in two shades of terracotta.

Lampshade

A grubby lampshade has been given a new lease of life by sponging with mushroom emulsion paint, leaving it to dry before sponging gold sea horses all around the edge.

Saucer

Unglazed ceramic takes stamps very successfully – this saucer is stamped with daisy sections.

Picture frame

A wooden frame has been given a colourwash before being stamped with lino cuts of stars and flashes.

Jug

A small jug is stamped on its unglazed surface using white quarter daisies with yellow centres.

CONTAINERS

All homes have containers of one sort or another ranging from boxes to bins and tins and jars. All of these can be easily decorated by stamping. They can be ready bought or custom made to suit your requirements and many companies sell boxes and other containers for storing items. Yet why buy one when we are surrounded by surplus packaging; why not make use of what you are given and customize it by painting on a base colour and then stamping? For example, shoe boxes are great for storing items such as photographs, holiday memories and old cheque books. Large cardboard boxes can be used to store clothing not in use this season.

CACTUS-STAMPED MUJI BOX

Rubber stationery stamps can be used to good effect on larger objects. This particular cardboard drawer unit was dull and brown, and very utilitarian in style. Brightly coloured paint and quirky stamps personalize objects boldly and simply.

1 Remove the drawers from the surround and mask off the canvas handles with the masking tape. Then paint the drawer faces with two coats of dark green emulsion, allowing the first coat of paint to dry before painting the second coat.

VARIATIONS

Instead of stamping randomly all over the box, consider grouping the cactus stamps together in threes, perhaps with the middle one jutting up slightly higher than the other two.

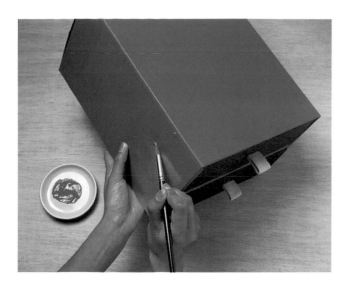

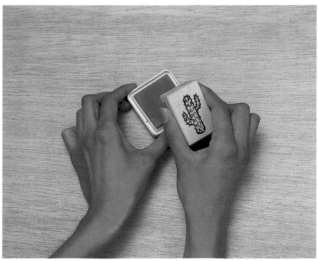

2 Paint the surround with the orange emulsion paint. Again, paint a couple of coats, allowing the first coat to dry before painting the second. Paint the front of the box before putting the drawers back in.

3 To apply ink to the stamp, press the stamp face down very firmly onto the orange ink pad. Alternatively, wipe the stamp over the surface of the pad. Practise stamping on scrap paper before working on the box so that you can get a feel of the stamp.

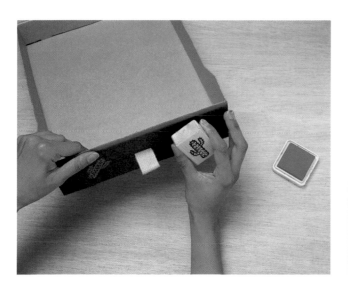

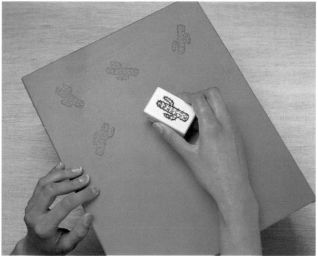

4 Once you are comfortable with the stamp, stamp the front of each green drawer with the orange ink. Here just two stamps were used on each drawer, each slanting in a slightly different direction.

5 Meticulously clean off the orange stamp ink from the cactus with a damp cloth or sponge. Then apply the green ink in the same way and randomly stamp all over the box.

TERRACOTTA FLOWERPOTS

A bright and colourful design can be made by using only one stamp with more than one colour, and by painting only part of the block, the design can be altered. The designs shown here have been stamped using very bright coloured emulsion paints - and paint was only applied to half the block.

1 Measure the circumference of each pot and make paper collars to fit around them — these will be your practice areas. Then, using the paintbrush, paint emulsion colours onto the section of the stamp that you wish to print.

VARIATIONS

Select alternative emulsion colours for a different effect — here, we have used combinations of blue, yellow and green.

2 Stamp the design onto the paper template to see how it will look on the pot. If you do not like the pattern, you can try something else on another collar without making a mess of the flowerpot. If you are changing colours on the block, wash off the paint in warm water, using a nail brush to ensure all the crevices are clean; pat dry with a clean cloth and then reapply paints and try out the design once more.

3 Apply more paint to the block and, holding it firmly against the flowerpot, roll it from one side to the other without lifting it from the surface of the pot. Now lift off the stamp, being careful not to smudge the paint.

4 Turn the block through 180 degrees so that the pattern is turned around, add more paint, and repeat step 3. Continue in this way, adding more paint to the block as you go, until the base of the flowerpot is covered with the design. If necessary, neaten the stamp prints with the paintbrush.

5 For the top rims, paint just a small portion of the stamp and make a pattern around the top edge of the flowerpot to make a border. Stamp a complete daisy on the base of the pot, too, if you wish.

SWIRLY STAMPED WINDOW BOX

If you know what colour flowers you will be putting into your window box, you can choose to stamp it with complementary colours. A nice idea is to use the same stamp throughout and change the colours as you go along. Come summertime, you will have a profusion of glorious colours filling your windowledge.

VARIATIONS

For a seaside box, paint it all over with a pale blue wash and use the same image in dark blue, but across the panels to form overlapping waves. Alternatively, an autumnal box can be created by stamping leaves in browns, ochres and yellows.

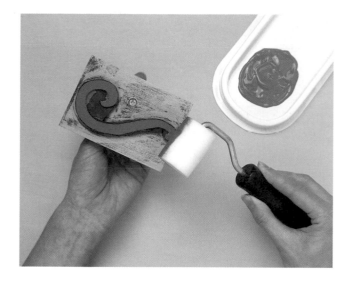

1 Using the roller, cover the surface of the swirl stamp evenly with pink emulsion paint. It is easier to get an even coverage on a larger stamp like this one by using a roller. Pour some of the paint into a plastic tray or a saucer and roll the roller through the paint ensuring an even coverage.

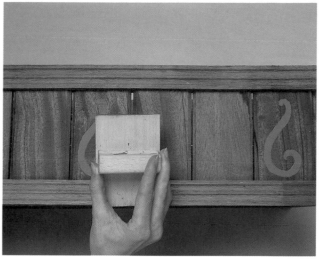

2 Press the stamp down firmly onto the first slat of the window box, pressing the stamp to make sure that the entire image has been transferred. Then lift the stamp off swiftly to avoid smudging. Repeat the same stamping operation on every third slat.

3 Using the damp cloth or sponge, clean off the stamp meticulously. Use the nail brush to ensure you get every last bit of paint off the stamp. Then cover the stamp with the green emulsion paint and stamp on the second slat. Repeat on every third slat after that.

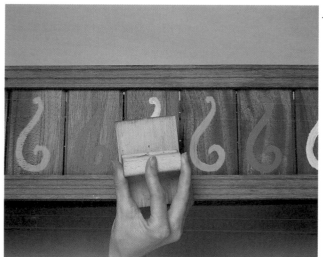

4 Clean off the stamp, again, and this time cover the stamp evenly with yellow paint ready to stamp on the remaining slats. To finish off the box, paint the top and bottom grooves with white emulsion, as in the photograph opposite. Sand down any uneven edges when the paint is dry.

CONTAINERS GALLERY

Busy bees
A small round box is painted in turquoise emulsion and then stamped with bees in contrasting yellow.

Shoe boxes
These are great for storing lots of items. Paint them white to cover up the labels before painting bright colours over the top and decorating them with lino prints.

Seed packet container
Needing to find a box to store all those half-used packets of seeds I came upon the perfect answer: a boring brown cardboard box. I gave it a new lease of life with some red paint and a carrot stamp.

Shaker boxes
These boxes have been painted fuchsia pink and then stamped with the traditional shaker symbol of the hand and heart.

Waste-paper bin

This bin is made from card and has been painted bright yellow on the outside with a large spot design in red stamped on it using a foam lid from a box of pins. The colours are reversed on the inside of the bin.

Serving tray

The brightly contrasting orange and green paints on this tray have a modern looking cactus design stamped on the lid.

STATIONERY

Whether it is writing paper, envelopes, or gift tags, stationery can be decorated to great advantage using stamps. Children's stationery can be made by using pretty stamps in bright colours. A border is effective on a piece of writing paper, and a single motif on the back of an envelope is rather attractive. Ordinary, inexpensive stationery can be uplifted and made special by using a stamp, and, sometimes, old printer's blocks can be found and used as modern stamps. This is particularly good if you can find letters because you can then stamp your initials on your stationery. Stamp on sticky labels to make book plates, or make decorative labels for jam jars of home produce.

FLEUR-DE-LYS BOX FILE

The fleur-de-lys is a very popular and striking image, especially for the festive season. Here it is used with black emulsion and white acrylic paints to give an otherwise plain cardboard box file a touch of class.

1 Open the flat box file right out and cover it completely with the black emulsion paint. Allow the first coat to dry and then paint on a second. Leave this one to dry too.

— VARIATIONS —

This fleur-de-lys stamp is a bought one and there are a wide range of different designs available. But why don't you cut your own out of a potato, cork or sponge (see pages 10-12) so that your file is unique.

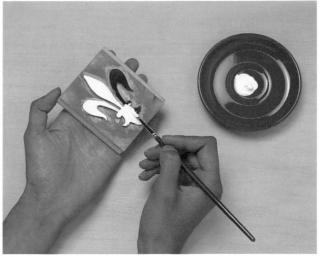

2 To mark out the box to position the stamps, first measure the width of the stamp with a ruler, and then measure along the base edges of the box file. With the pencil, mark off how many stamps will fit along the edge. On this particular file, three fleur-de-lys images fitted along each side and one was centred neatly on the back.

3 Using the fine paintbrush and white acrylic paint, cover the stamp surface as evenly as possible. Too much paint on one area will result in an uneven print being made when it comes to the stamping.

4 Stamp down the fleur-de-lys firmly where you have marked off the spaces. A box file like this is made of corrugated cardboard, making the surface slightly bouncy, so ensure that you press down very firmly, and at the same time rock the stamp to and fro. Repeat until you have completed your pattern, painting on more paint between each stamp.

5 Because of the uneven surface of corrugated cardboard, you may find the stamps are uneven. If necessary, now is the time to touch up the fleur-de-lys, using the white acrylic paint and fine paintbrush.

DAISY ENVELOPES

Customize and personalize your own and your child's stationery by stamping small prints onto paper and envelopes alike. The designs can range from tiny black prints on sophisticated cartridge paper to brightly coloured daisies, like those on the envelopes stamped here.

YOU WILL NEED

Daisy stamp

Acrylic paints (pink, green)

Paintbrush (fine)

Plain envelopes

VARIATIONS

On the writing paper, a border has been stamped all the way around, but it would be just as interesting to stamp down just one side, say, or along the bottom edge. The end result would be nicely understated.

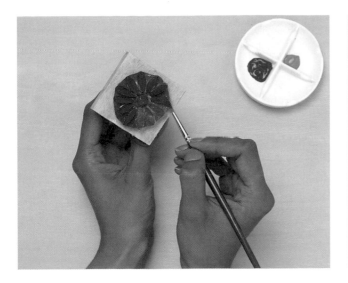

1 Holding the daisy stamp steady, carefully paint the petals using the pink acrylic paint. Use the fine paintbrush to do this as it means you will be less likely to smudge the paint.

2 Clean the paintbrush in warm water and then paint the centre of the flower with the green acrylic paint. Make sure that the paint is the right thickness for stamping, by testing the stamp on scrap paper first.

3 Decide on where you wish to stamp the daisy and press the stamp down firmly, rocking it ever so slightly from side to side to ensure that the whole image is transferred. Lift the stamp swiftly and in one smooth movement to avoid smudging.

4 You may find that the stamped image is uneven in places. If so, paint over any part of the petals or the centre that you wish to tidy up with the same paintbrush.

POTATO-PRINTED WRAPPING PAPER

Creating a stunning gift wrap paper is easier than it seems: this paper started life as plain brown packaging paper and a potato. Potato prints allow you to carve your own stamp designs, making your stamps unique and individual. However, remember that the simpler your design, the bolder your stamped image will be.

1 Cut a potato in half, lengthways, so that you get the largest possible surface on which to carve your design. Take just one half of the potato, and place the circular object onto it to use as a template, a small jar lid is ideal for this purpose. Then use the sharp knife to cut around the lid carefully. Cut about 12 mm (½ in) deep making sure not to cut straight through the potato.

YOU WILL NEED

Large potato
Sharp knife
Round object to use as a template, eg lid
Kitchen paper
Stamping paint (cream)
Paintbrush (fine)
Brown packaging paper

— VARIATIONS —

Don't feel obliged to stick with one colour for the stamps on wrapping paper. Alternate colours across the rows, or just mix them up any old how. Bright poster paints can be mixed into a whole rainbow of colours.

2 To make the circle stand proud, carefully trim away the excess potato. Use the same knife and slowly slice around the potato paring off the pieces of potato that lie outside the circle.

3 Before applying the paint, pat the potato dry on a piece of kitchen paper. Then paint the potato stamp with the stamping paint, applying the paint quite thickly with the paintbrush.

4 Place the stamp onto the brown packaging paper and press down firmly, taking care not to let the stamp slide. To avoid smudging the paint, lift the stamp off in one movement.

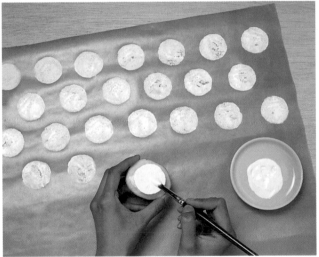

5 Repeat stamping like this until you achieve the pattern that you desire adding more paint to the potato between each stamp. The pattern made here is created by stamping the circles in lines across the paper, until the paper is full.

STATIONERY GALLERY

Writing paper and envelopes
By purchasing relatively inexpensive writing paper and envelopes and printing a border design a designer look can be achieved for next to nothing.

Note paper
The leaf design used on the recycled note paper and envelopes is a modern polymer block.

Gift tags
A hole punch, some string and a single stamp make personalized gift tags.

Birthday cards
It can be difficult to find just the right card for someone. The design here is for a Pisces friend. It is a simple lino cut, printed in one colour.

Storage drawer unit
A boring cardboard drawer unit has great appeal when it is painted and stamped with a pair of retro 1950s Grace Kelly sunglasses.

Gift boxes
The little black and white gift boxes are stamped with a single motif on each side. They are great for tiny presents.

GIFTS FOR CHILDREN

Children like stamped images and they also love to stamp. All items from furniture to friezes can be stamped, including toy boxes, toys and tee-shirts. Children's toy shops sell ready-made stamps in rubber which often come in kit form with a handle and base into which different stamps may be fixed. Likewise, toy departments sell cut shapes in sponge which may be used for stamping on larger items such as walls or furniture. When stamping for children you are likely to find, as I did, that you are stamping with children. This craft is so easy, everyone wants to join in.

CORK STAMPED LAMP

A cork is a very simple and effective way of stamping, giving an unsophisticated and yet attractive look to the stamped image. The lamp and base here are stamped in contrasting red and white.

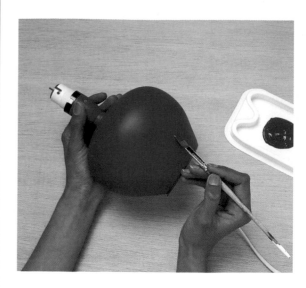

1 Remove the shade from the base and then paint the lamp base with three or four coats of the red emulsion. This many coats gives a smooth and even colour to the base. Allow the paint to dry between the layers.

YOU WILL NEED

Standard lamp (white)

Emulsion paints (red, white)

Paintbrush (fine)

Two corks, with smooth ends

VARIATIONS

Don't paint the lamp base red, keep it white and stamp it with the same colour as the lampshade, or stamp the shade and base with two different colours, but both on white backgrounds.

2 Take one of the corks and paint the end with the same red emulsion that you have just been using. You might need to put on quite alot of paint to begin with as it will initially soak into the cork.

3 Placing one hand on the back of the surface you are working on to support the shade, press the paint-covered cork onto the shade. To ensure a complete shape when the cork is removed, rotate the wrist that is holding the cork.

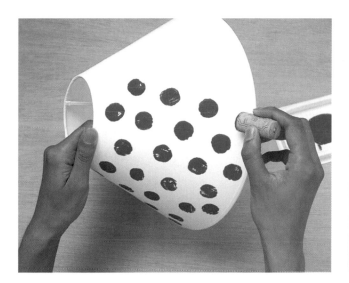

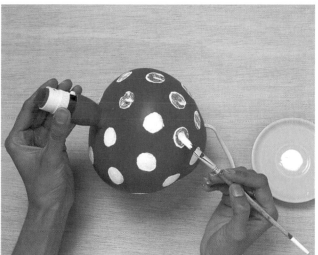

4 Repeat this step randomly all over the shade, painting the cork at every second or third stamp. Rather than working around the shade in rows, it is easiest to work from the top to the bottom on each portion as this means you don't have to keep on turning the shade around all the time.

5 Paint the second cork with the white emulsion and stamp the base in the same manner as you did the shade. To give a smoother finish, touch up the stamps on the base with white emulsion and a paintbrush. The cork stamps on the shade, however, actually look better when they are left to look natural.

GALLOPING HORSES RIBBON

All little girls love horses and they also love to wear ribbons in their hair. To stamp images onto ribbon is very simple, although the kind of ribbon you use is important. The recommended ribbon to stamp onto is the transluscent ribbon used here or a single-backed satin ribbon. On the double-backed ribbon the stamped image does tend to bleed so it is best to avoid this.

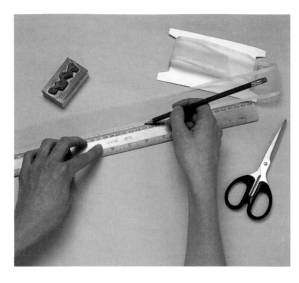

1 Take a length of ribbon, then by measuring the length of the stamp and how many stamps you require on the ribbon cut it to the right size. Press using the iron set at a medium temperature.

YOU WILL NEED

Length of transluscent ribbon (cream)

Pencil

Ruler

Sharp scissors

Iron

Galloping horses stamp

Stamping ink pad (plum)

SAFETY NOTE
If you are stamping ribbons for very young children, ensure that the paints you use are non-toxic.

--- VARIATIONS ---

Group the horses together so that there is a space between each 'herd'. Or have brown, black and white horses galloping across the ribbon.

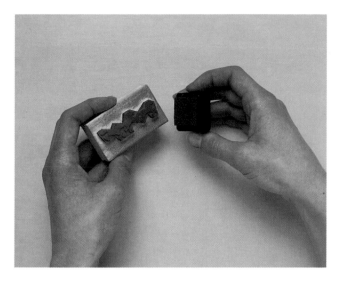

2 Apply the stamping ink to the galloping horses stamp, by either tapping the stamp onto the ink pad or by wiping the ink pad over the stamp. Make sure the ink is applied evenly all over the stamp.

3 Place the stamp onto the ribbon and press it down firmly, rocking it slightly from side to side to ensure that the whole image is transferred onto the ribbon. Some of the ink may pass through the ribbon so protect your worksurface with a layer of newspaper or sheet of cardboard.

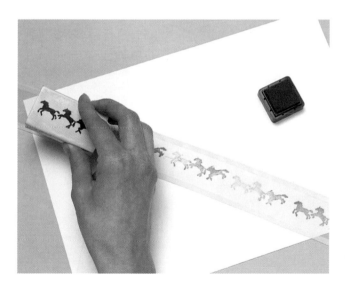

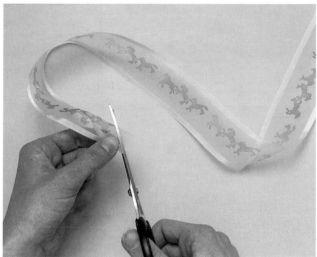

4 Continue to stamp the horses along the ribbon placing each subsequent stamp at the end of the previously completed one. For a consistently-coloured ribbon, put on more ink for each stamp; for some variation, stamp two or three images before adding more ink.

5 To finish off the ribbon neatly and to prevent fraying, take each end of the ribbon and use the scissors to snip out a triangle so that there is a "V" at each end. For a simpler end, just cut off some of the ribbon at an angle.

PLANES AND CLOUDS CUPBOARD

Sponge shapes are available in toy shops and they make great stamps. Unlike more conventional sponging, however, you need to push down the sponge quite firmly. In this way you make sure that the shape doesn't smudge, and that there is a definite image with a sharp outline when the sponge is lifted.

1 Paint the cabinet with a layer of white emulsion and using the wider paintbrush. Leave the paint to dry, wash out the paintbrush thoroughly and then apply two coats of the bright yellow emulsion paint.

YOU WILL NEED

Bedside cabinet

Emulsion paints (white, yellow)

Paintbrushes (5 cm [2 in]-wide, sturdy and fine artist's)

Sponge lid from a pin box or a round piece of sponge

Acrylic paints (white, blue)

Aeroplane-shaped sponge

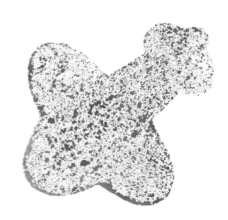

— VARIATIONS —

Add decorations to the planes once the stamps have dried. Some could have dots added to them, others wavy lines, each in strong, contrasting colours.

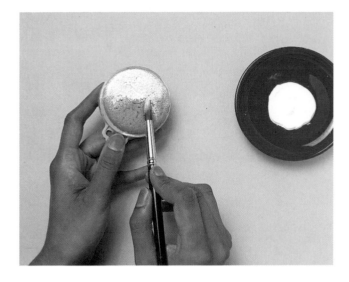

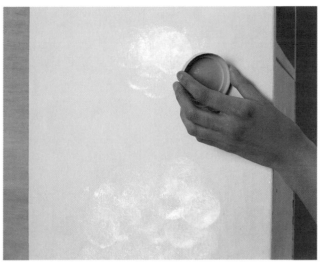

2 To make the clouds, paint the round sponge quite thickly with the white acrylic paint, applying the paint wth the sturdy artist's paintbrush. Pat off excess paint onto a piece of scrap paper and then apply the paint onto the cupboard.

3 Pat down the sponge gently so that the stamped image is soft with no definite lines, and make the cloud shape by stamping the sponge images in a clockwise direction. Fill in the centre after you have finished the surround.

4 Wash the sturdy paintbrush thoroughly and then paint the aeroplane-shaped sponge with the blue acrylic paint. Stamp it onto the cupboard, randomly, making sure that the transferred images are sharp. If they aren't, touch them up with the fine paintbrush.

5 Wash the sturdy paintbrush thoroughly once again and then use the round sponge and the white acrylic paint once more to stamp cloud trails behind the plane shapes to finish off.

GINGHAM BAG

Gingham fabric comes in bright, cheerful colours — predominantly blue, red and yellow — and it is the ideal fabric for a children's bedroom, whether for curtains, a quilt cover or, as here, a handy bag for putting things in. The red star stamped all over it adds a very attractive decoration.

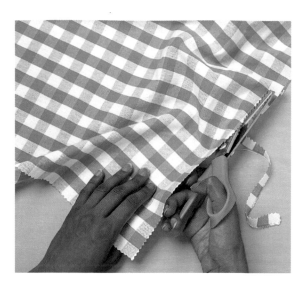

1 Cut a piece of gingham to the width of the finished bag plus 5 cm (2 in) seam allowances, and twice the desired length. Press the fabric so that it is smooth when being stamped on.

YOU WILL NEED
Gingham fabric
Dressmaker's scissors
Pencil
Star stamp
Paintbrush
Fabric paint (red)
Cotton thread
Ribbon

VARIATIONS

Make stars of all colours — don't feel obliged to stick to one colour, like here. Alternatively, stamp onto every white square but in alternate rows, leaving every other row blank.

2 To prevent confusion when printing, mark every square with a faint pencil dot where you are going to print. Do this on the right side of the fabric and then lay out the fabric ready to be stamped on.

3 Paint the fabric paint onto the motif using the paintbrush. Then place the motif above the first square where you wish the colour to be dark and carefully apply it.

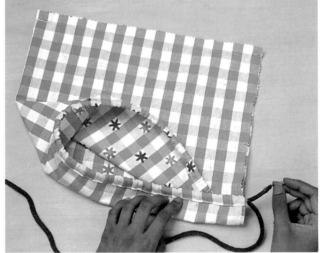

4 Without repainting the motif, stamp it into the next square. In this way you will get a pattern of light and dark motifs. Continue stamping the star across the bag in the same way.

5 Make up the bag by folding it in half with the right sides together and the fold at the bottom of the bag. Then sew up the sides with a neat running stitch. At the top of the bag make a casing for the ribbon by folding over the top twice and stitching it in place leaving a gap for the ribbon to be inserted. Thread the ribbon through to finish the bag — use a safety pin at the end to help it — and finally turn the right sides out.

GIFTS FOR CHILDREN GALLERY

Tulip frieze
Wall friezes can be expensive, but this one wasn't. It was made by cutting lining paper, painting it with emulsion, and stamping on a design from cut potatoes.

Cushion covers
Potatoes were cut into simple geometric shapes which were then stamped using bright fabric paints onto ticking. The fabric was then made into cushion covers.

Child's chair
Painted bright blue, the chair has been stamped with a lino cut tiny star, a polymer medium star and a sponge cheese-textured crescent moon.

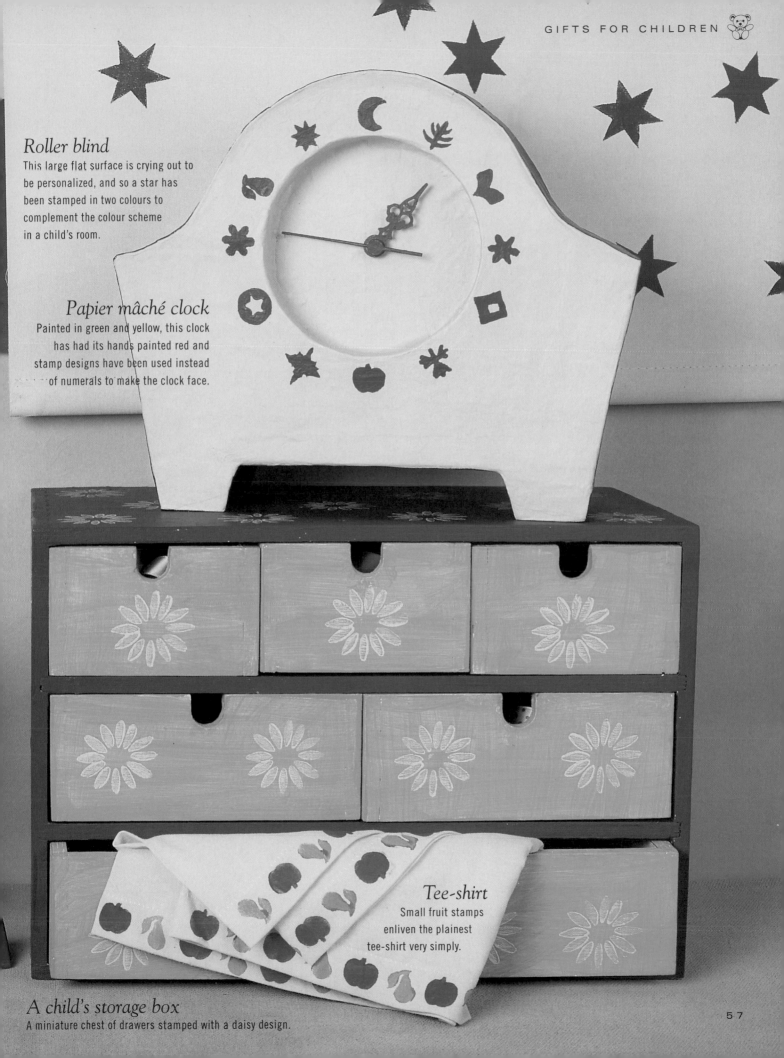

Roller blind
This large flat surface is crying out to be personalized, and so a star has been stamped in two colours to complement the colour scheme in a child's room.

Papier mâché clock
Painted in green and yellow, this clock has had its hands painted red and stamp designs have been used instead of numerals to make the clock face.

Tee-shirt
Small fruit stamps enliven the plainest tee-shirt very simply.

A child's storage box
A miniature chest of drawers stamped with a daisy design.

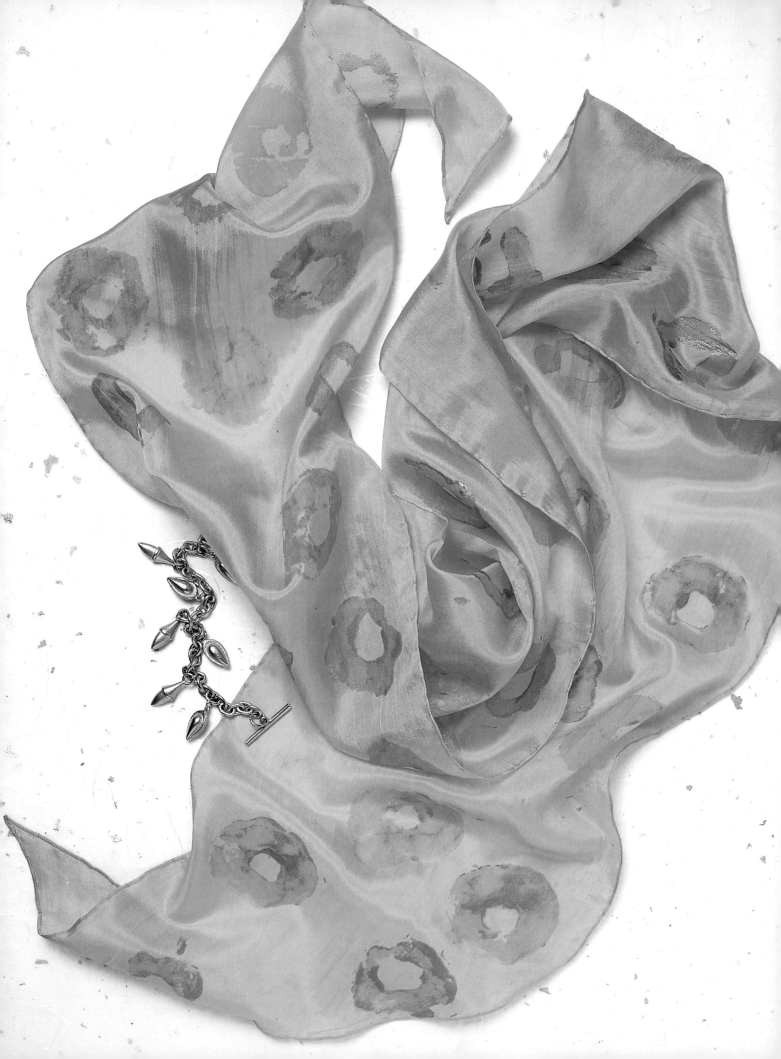

GIFTS FOR ADULTS

The items in this chapter are personal things that you might make for yourself or would like to give as a present. We have included clothing such as shoes and a scarf. The scarf was printed using a dried apple ring; a picture album was stamped using a simple wooden block imported from India, and a notebook for gardeners personalized by stamping on garden implements. If you cannot get hold of the exact stamps we have used, make your own by cutting lino or vegetables to make a print (see pages 11-12). By stamping your personality onto a gift you are making an object to be cherished.

FISH PHOTOGRAPH ALBUM

On the recycled cover of this photograph album, a hand-carved wooden stamp has been used repeatedly to create an effective pattern in monochrome.

1 Measure how long the fish stamp is and work out how many times it will fit across the cover so that you can plan your pattern. Carefully mark off the positions of the stamp with the pencil and ruler.

VARIATIONS

Instead of having the fishes swimming neatly in rows across the front of this photograph album, perhaps they could be swimming in shoals, or a group of them following a lone fish somewhere out front. The beauty of stamping is that you can be very free and easy with your design ideas. It is always worth experimenting on scraps of paper beforehand.

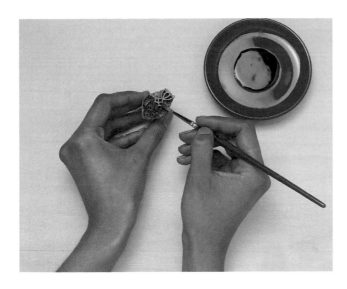

2 Paint the fish stamp with the black stamping paint, and using the fine paintbrush. Before printing with the stamp, check that there are no air bubbles visible; these will make the stamps uneven.

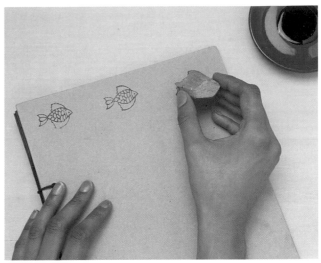

3 Stamp the fish onto the cover where you have marked off. Press down the stamp firmly to ensure a solid outline and lift directly off the paper to avoid smudging.

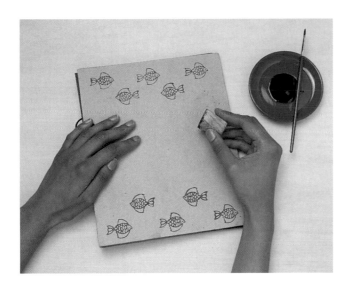

4 Repeat stamping the fish until the pattern you require has been achieved. Add more paint to the stamp each time to ensure that you make consistent prints across the photograph album.

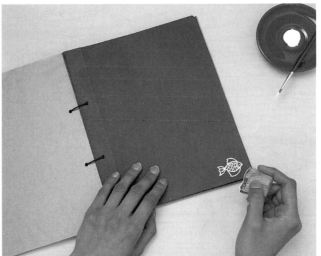

5 Clean the stamp and paintbrush thoroughly. It is best to do this by rinsing them out under a running tap, scrubbing the stamp with the nail brush. Once you have dried off the stamp, paint it white and then stamp the lower right-hand corner of each page, allowing each page to dry before turning onto the next.

CORK TABLE MATS

Just as cork is a simple medium to stamp with, it is excellent for receiving a stamped design. Cork table mats are crying out to be stamped on and with this simple string method you can create all sorts of different designs.

1 Cut a shape from the cardboard to exactly the same size as the cork mat. Simply place the mat on the cardboard, draw around it with a pencil and then cut. If you are using plywood, draw around the mat and then stick the string down within this outline. Unless you have a jigsaw to hand, there is no need to cut out the shape. Cover the cardboard in glue.

YOU WILL NEED

Cork mats
Cardboard or plywood
Pencil
Scissors
Glue
String
Emulsion paint (black)
Paintbrush
Varnish (gloss or matt)

— VARIATIONS —

All manner of patterns can be made with the string ranging from zigzags to Greek keys. For a design that needs to be regularly spaced it is best to draw the pattern onto the cardboard with a pencil before sticking the string in place. In this way, you can easily make changes by rubbing out and starting again.

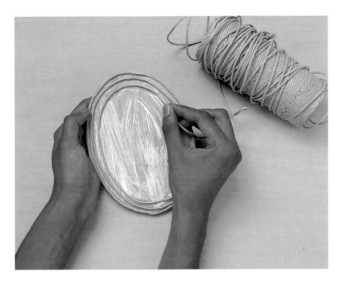

2 Stick down the string in one long spiral onto the printing board. Press it down firmly so that the string is stuck to the board very well and then leave the board to dry.

3 Apply the emulsion paint onto the string using the paintbrush. Use only small quantities of paint at a time so that it doesn't fill up the spaces between the string too much.

4 Place the stringed board on top of the cork mat and then press it firmly all over. Lift the board off and a string image is on the mat. For each further mat that you are going to stamp, repaint the string to retain a good, strong image.

5 To finish off each mat, paint the edges with the same colour. Then leave to dry and paint on several coats of varnish to act as a sealant. Leave each coat to dry before adding the next one.

GIFTS FOR ADULTS GALLERY

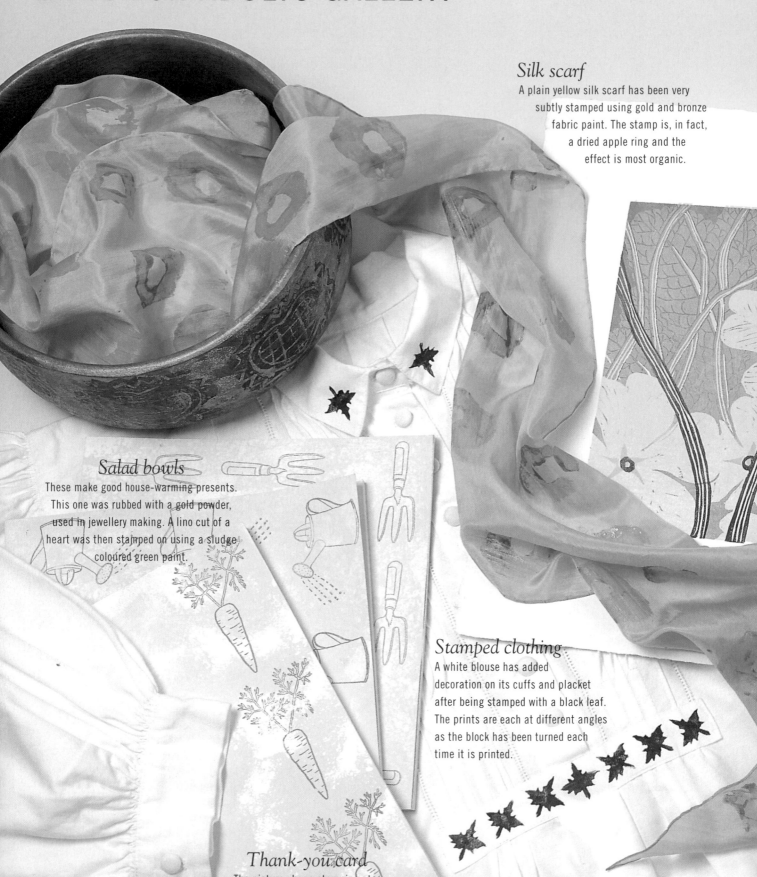

Silk scarf
A plain yellow silk scarf has been very subtly stamped using gold and bronze fabric paint. The stamp is, in fact, a dried apple ring and the effect is most organic.

Salad bowls
These make good house-warming presents. This one was rubbed with a gold powder, used in jewellery making. A lino cut of a heart was then stamped on using a sludge coloured green paint.

Stamped clothing
A white blouse has added decoration on its cuffs and placket after being stamped with a black leaf. The prints are each at different angles as the block has been turned each time it is printed.

Thank-you card
The picture shows stamping at a larger scale: it is a lino cut, printed in two colours.

Folk art cupboard

The design on the cupboard of folk art birds and hearts has been made by building up the design using a variety of different stamps.

Stamped shoes

Rather dull brown suede espadrilles have been decorated for a beach holiday with a stamp of a large sea shell.

Paper lampshade

The fleur-de-lys is a popular motif and it has been used here with great effect on a paper lampshade.

GIFTS FOR SPECIAL OCCASIONS

Special occasions include Christmas, Easter, Valentine's day, Mother's day, Father's day, and – if you wish – baby brother's day. This again is an opportunity to make a personalized gift. It is the time to make inexpensive decorations, stamp birth signs on paper table napkins, or onto Christmas candles. Specialist paper decorations can be expensive but by cutting lining paper and using a swede you can make and stamp a frieze for Hallowe'en, Christmas, that special birthday, or any other occasion. If you are suddenly presented with an unexpected birthday to celebrate and no card or wrapping paper, you can stamp your own stylish paper with little more than a potato and brown wrapping paper.

VALENTINE CARD

This valentine card is more sophisticated than most and it manages to employ a humble polystyrene wall tile to make a pattern. The end result is a delightful swirly design complemented by hand-painted dots of red paint along the top and bottom of the card.

1 Draw a heart template onto the scrap paper and cut it out using the scissors. Place the template on the polystyrene tile, draw around it and then cut out the heart shape using the craft knife and cutting mat.

YOU WILL NEED

Scrap paper
Pencil
Scissors
Textured polystyrene tile
Craft knife
Cutting mat
Tissue paper (white)
Emulsion or acrylic paint (red)
Roller
Cartridge paper (off-white)
Glue
Paintbrush (fine)

—— VARIATIONS ——

If you prefer, cut the heart stamp as a smaller one and stamp it onto four pieces of tissue paper. These can then be stuck in place, one in each corner of the cartridge paper card.

2 Next, draw around the template onto the tissue paper. Carefully rip out the heart shape including a border around the pencilled outline. The end result will be a heart shape that is slightly larger than the polystyrene stamp.

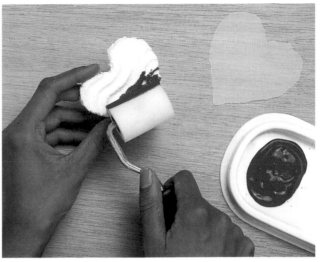

3 Pour some of the red emulsion or acrylic paint into a saucer, or similar container, and roll the roller across the paint until it is evenly covered. Then pass the roller over the stamp to transfer the paint, and press the stamp firmly onto the tissue paper.

4 Leave the tissue paper to dry. While this is happening, fold the cartridge paper in half to make a card and then glue the tissue paper heart onto it making sure the heart is centred and vertical.

5 To finish off the card, add some decorative details. Here, two rows of dots have been painted along the top and bottom edges using the fine paintbrush. In the picture opposite you can see that the card that is just visible at the back has small dots painted around the heart as a variation.

HALLOWE'EN FRIEZE

Friezes like this are incredibly quick and simple to make — just right for a one-off occasion like Hallowe'en. For large designs like this pumpkin face, a swede is the ideal vegetable for stamping with.

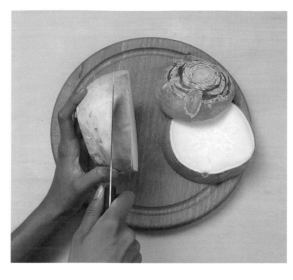

1 Cut the swede in half. Then trace the templates on pages 76 and 77 and transfer them, one to each half of the cut swede. Do this by laying the tracing paper over the swede and cut through the lines with the craft knife.

— VARIATIONS —

In place of either the pumpkin or bat, make your own witch's hat stamp — this is particularly easy to cut from a swede as it has such a simple outline.

2 Carefully cut out the design using the craft knife. Cut around the edges first and then carefully cut out slithers of swede from the more detailed parts, such as the eyes and mouth.

3 Cut the lining paper to the depth you would like the frieze to be and paint it orange. To achieve the above paint effect, load the paintbrush with paint and then dip it in some water before transferring it onto the lining paper. In this way the degrees of colour intensity will vary. Leave the paint to dry.

4 First stamp on the pumpkin images. Using the black paint, paint the pumpkin face on the swede and then stamp along the frieze. Add paint to the swede between each stamp to retain a consistent printed image.

5 Using black paint again, stamp the bats onto the frieze. Position them between, above and below the pumpkin faces and let them fly at different angles by rotating the swede as you stamp.

EMBOSSED CHRISTMAS DECORATIONS

Embossing is a stamping technique with an amazing result. Here, for a festive feel, Christmas decorations are made by embossing cartridge paper with copper and silver powder. They are then cut out to make small shapes suitable for hanging from a tree.

1 Using the black ink pad and either the fleur-de-lys or paisley stamps (here, we used the fleur-de-lys one), stamp the image onto the cartridge paper. Apply the ink to the stamp by tapping the stamp onto the ink pad or wiping the ink pad over the stamp.

YOU WILL NEED

Stamping ink pad (black)
Fleur-de-lys stamp
Paisley stamp
Cartridge paper
Embossing powder (copper, silver)
Paintbrush (fine)
Heat source (iron or toaster)
Scissors
Coloured card
Glue
Hole punch
Ribbon

— VARIATIONS —

Make gift tags in the same way but you only need to glue a single image to the coloured card so that there is space on the back for your message and name.

2 While the image is still wet, sprinkle the embossing powder (here, we used the copper powder) all over it. Shake off the excess powder onto a clean piece of paper and, if necessary, use the small paintbrush to remove any stubborn excess powder.

3 Hold the embossed cartridge paper above the heat source until the powder melts onto the paper. This will take a few minutes and the end result is a raised, metallic image.

4 To make each decoration, you will need two images, one for each side, but make sure that you have a reversible design. The paisley motifs opposite would work for one-sided decorations only. Cut around each embossed image, leaving a small border, and also cut out the coloured card to your required shape, remembering to allow a space at the top for a hole. Then glue the cut out embossed images onto both sides of the coloured card and leave to dry.

5 Using the hole punch, punch a hole into the top of the card. Then thread the ribbon through this hole, tie a knot at the top and hang the decoration on your Christmas tree, or, say, a series of them across a window.

GIFTS FOR SPECIAL OCCASIONS GALLERY

Wrapping paper
Red wrapping paper with a fibre running through it has been stamped with a heart design in gold. To make a pretty parcel it was tied with gold and red ribbon with added hearts.

Candles
The candles have been stamped with a golden star design using stamping paint. When stamping on wax, it is worth experimenting with different paints as some of them will not dry and just smudge.

Festive napkin holders and napkins
Suitable for parties, these can be made from cardboard tubes which are covered in a layer of papier mâché, then painted blue and stamped with a simple gold star design. Navy paper napkins have been stamped with signs of the zodiac.

Wrapping ribbon
Grosgrain ribbon has been cut with pointed ends and then stamped with a heart at each end.

Voile curtain

A voile curtain is made to look special by stamping golden suns, moons and stars all over it at random.

Pin cushion

This pin cushion was stamped with a fleur-de-lys. It makes a pretty mother's day, or birthday present. The edges of the stamped image have been dotted with pearl beads and pins.

Cracker

To make a mother's day wrapping paper, a rose design was cut from lino and stamped onto green paper. The present was then wrapped up to look like a cracker.

Candle shades

These have been stamped with a repeat paisley design which fits perfectly.

TEMPLATES

Lino stamps have been used in various projects throughout the book. To make your own lino prints like these, use a photocopier to enlarge or reduce the images as required. Place a piece of carbon paper, ink side down, on to a piece of lino and then place the photocopied image on top of the carbon paper. Trace over the photocopied image and through the carbon paper with a pen or pencil. Remove the carbon paper and photocopied image to reveal a carbon copy of your image. Using a pen go over the image on the lino to give a clearer idea of where to cut. Take a lino cutting tool and carefully cut out the image on the lino. Follow instructions for making a stamp on page 11.

Festive Napkin Holder
(see page 74)

Hallowe'en Frieze
(see page 70)

Wooden Fruit Bowl
(see page 64)

Flower
(see page 11)

Birthday Card
(see page 44)

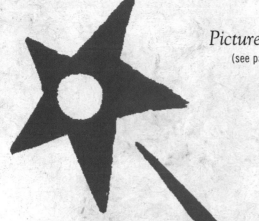

Picture Frame
(see page 28)

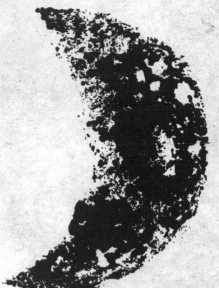

Child's Chair
(see page 56)

Wooden Chair with Bird
(see page 18)

Mackintosh Rose
(see page 75)

Hallowe'en Frieze
(see page 70)

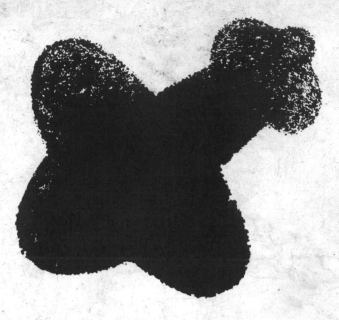

Planes and Clouds Cupboard
(see page 52)

Tulip Frieze
(see page 56)

Daisy Vase
(see page 16)

Valentine Card
(see page 68)

Tulip Frieze
(see page 56)

SUPPLIERS

If you are unable to find rubber stamping materials in your area, contact your local craft shop, as nearly all craft shops will order the materials specially for you.

UNITED KINGDOM

Fred Aldous Ltd
PO Box 37
Lever St
Manchester M60 1UX
Tel: 0161 236 2477
Fax: 0161 236 6075)
(fish transfers, linocutting kit and decoupage varnish)

The English Stamp Company
Sunnydown
Worth Matravers
Dorset
BH19 3JP
Tel: 01929 439117
(stamps, stamping paint and rollers)

Homestyle Stores
AG Stanley
Victoria Mills
Macclesfield Road
Homes Chapple
Cheshire
Tel: 01477 544544
(for suplying the lamp shade and base on page 48-9)

Globe Enterprises
23 Church Avenue
Pinner
Middx HA5 5JA
(wooden blocks, recycled paper and envelopes)

The Holding Company
243-245 Kings Road
London SW3 5EL
Tel: 0171 532 1600
(boxes on which to stamp and ink pads)

Inca Stamp
136 Stanley Green Road
Poole
Dorset
BH15 3AH
Tel: 01202 660080
(stamps, rollers and embossing powder)

Liquitex Paints
Binney and Smith (Eur.) Ltd
Ampthill Road
Bedford
MK42 9RS
Tel: 01234 360201
(paints)

CM Offray and Son
Fir Tree Place
Church Road
Ashford
Middx TW15 2PH
Tel: 01784 247281
(ribbons)

Philip and Tacey
Northway
Andover
Hampshire SP10 5BA
(fabric stamps and paints)

Prices Candles
110 York Road
London SW11 3RU
Tel: 0171 228 3345
(candles and candle shades)

SOUTH AFRICA

Anne's Arts and Crafts
6 Recreation Road
Fish Hoek, Cape Town
Tel: (021) 782 2061/782 3169
Fax: (021) 782 6268

Art Mates
Shop 313 Musgrave Centre
124 Musgrave Road
Durban
Tel: (031) 21 0094

Craftsman, The
Shop 10
Progress House
110 Bordeaux Drive
Randburg, Johannesburg
Tel: (011) 787 1846
Tel: (011) 886 0441

E Schweikerdt (Pty) Ltd
Vatika Centre
Cnr Muckleneuk and
Fehrsen Streets
Brooklyn, Pretoria
Tel: (021) 45 55406

E Schweikerdt (Pty) Ltd
590 Souter Street
Pretoria West
Tel: (012) 327 0708/9

E Schweikerdt (Pty) Ltd
Mail Order Service
PO Box 697
Pretoria 0001

Mycrafts Shop (Pte)
Aliwal Street
Bloemfontein
Tel: (051) 48 4119

Peers Handicrafts
35 Burg Street
Cape Town
Tel: (021) 24 2520

Southern Arts and Crafts
105 Main Street
Rosettenville, Johannesburg
Tel/Fax: (011) 683 6566

AUSTRALIA

Allen's Rubber Stamps
PO Box 283
Warkworth
Tel/Fax: (09) 357 0412

Auckland Rubber Stamps
Unit 2, 50 Stoddard Road
Mt Roskill
Auckland
Tel: (09) 629 2692

Dominion Paint Centre
227 Dominion Road
Mt Eden
Tel: (09) 638 7593

P A Inkman Ltd
36 Doulgas Street
Ponsonby
Aukland
Tel: (09) 638 7593

NEW ZEALAND

Arts & Crafts Corner
34 Mint Street
East Victoria Park
Western Australia 6101
Tel: (02) 221 5111

Boronia Arts & Crafts
Centre
247 Dorset Road
Boronia
Victoria 3155
Tel: (03) 762 1751

Craft Lovers
37 Murray Street
Tanunda
South Australia 5352
Tel: (08) 563 0504

Lincraft
Gallery Level, Imperial
Arcade
Pitt Street
Sydney NSW 2000
Tel: ((02) 221 5111

Sundale Handcrafts
16B Logan Village Shopping
Centre
Bryants Road
Loganholme
Queensland 4129
Tel: (07) 801 1121

INDEX

Page numbers in *italics* represent photographs